Kathleen Hackett
Creative Direction by Hilary Robertson
Photographs by Matthew Williams

Brooklyn Interiors

RIZZOLI
NEW YORK

New York Paris London Milan

Ad Hoc. Renegade. Freestyle.

"There's no best way to live, but Brooklyn comes pretty close."

This comes from Becca Abrams, who lives with her husband Nathan Benn and son Tobias in a condominium on the borough's waterfront (page 132), but any one of the people in this book might have said it. As I cast around for potential interiors to include on the following pages, visiting dozens of homes so graciously opened to me, it became evident that every owner roundly shares this sentiment.

Brooklynites have long had a reputation for marching to their own beat. Nowhere is this more obvious than behind the front doors of their brownstones, duplexes, condos, co-ops, lofts, walk-ups, floor-throughs, carriage houses, and railroad apartments. In Brooklyn, there are as many interior design approaches as there are people. The single common thread is a refusal—to follow the herd, to adopt trends, to strive for the neighbor's sofa. It's perfectly acceptable, however, to rescue a cast-off couch, as is the case in my own home (it starts things off on page 12), where a custom 9-foot-long beauty was bequeathed to us by a beloved neighbor who was downsizing. We upholstered it in a raisin silk velvet and voilà, it was ours. The spaces and places that follow evince this renegade spirit, one that reflects the idiosyncratic nature of the borough itself.

Around the world, style arbiters have ballyhooed the Brooklyn look— one that has come to be defined by reclaimed wood, bare light bulbs, exposed brick walls, and industrial furniture. It is a distinct look to be sure, but it is only a short chapter of the story. Brooklyn, it turns out, is not only a cultural melting pot—Agnethe Glatved and Matthew Septimus (page 222) love their Ditmas Park neighborhood for the twenty different languages spoken at the local elementary school—but it's also a bastion of design diversity espoused by indie fashion designers, filmmakers, photographers, artists, writers, actors, and entrepreneurs. Their aesthetics vary as wildly as their work does; there are minimalists, magpies, and monks among them.

During the stage in producing this book devoted to putting words to images, I realized how much affection I felt for every single person in it. I was drawn to them for their attachment to their surroundings and the soulfulness with which they talked about their homes, and that connection was only deepened once they let me take a peek inside. When Merele Williams talks about living through a gut renovation of the brownstone she shared with her late husband, the artist Terry Adkins, the home (page 108) became far more than a homage to his work; it tells the story of a woman's determination to continue a tradition of art and music that was so important to her spouse. My hope is that you will find inspiration not only in the way these Brooklynites live in their homes, but in the spirit with which they do it. It is interior design at its most vital and clever. —Kathleen Hackett, Brooklyn, New York, 2015

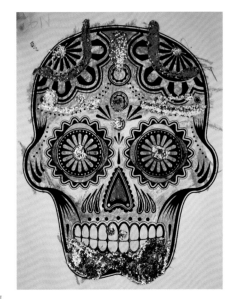

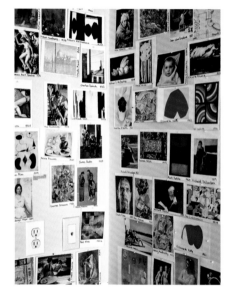

Plastered

Stephen Antonson & Kathleen Hackett, Boerum Hill

There was nothing charming about the brick row house Stephen Antonson and Kathleen Hackett moved into several years ago—apart from the company it kept on a handsome tree-lined street. It seemed that the mission of the former owner, who had lived there for almost forty years, was to rid the place of anything that required care and maintenance. Character was among the most serious casualties, but the pair knew they could handily build it back up.

Put plaster of Paris and paint in the right hands and even the most banal spaces can be transformed. Antonson, an artist and designer whose plaster furnishings, lighting, and accessories are sought after by A-list interior designers around the world, can't help but bring his work home. "He is quite compulsive in general, but it works out to be a lovely compulsion, because we've ended up with a house filled with beautiful pieces Stephen's made himself," says Hackett. Antonson admits, however, that his passion can at times border on obsession. When his wife and two sons were away one summer, he decided to paint an elaborate labyrinthine pattern on the deeply unappealing hallway floor. He sketched it using miles of painter's tape in the method of Harold with his purple crayon. "That was the fun part. It was like making a painting on the floor, but within the confines of architecture," says Antonson.   —Matt Austin

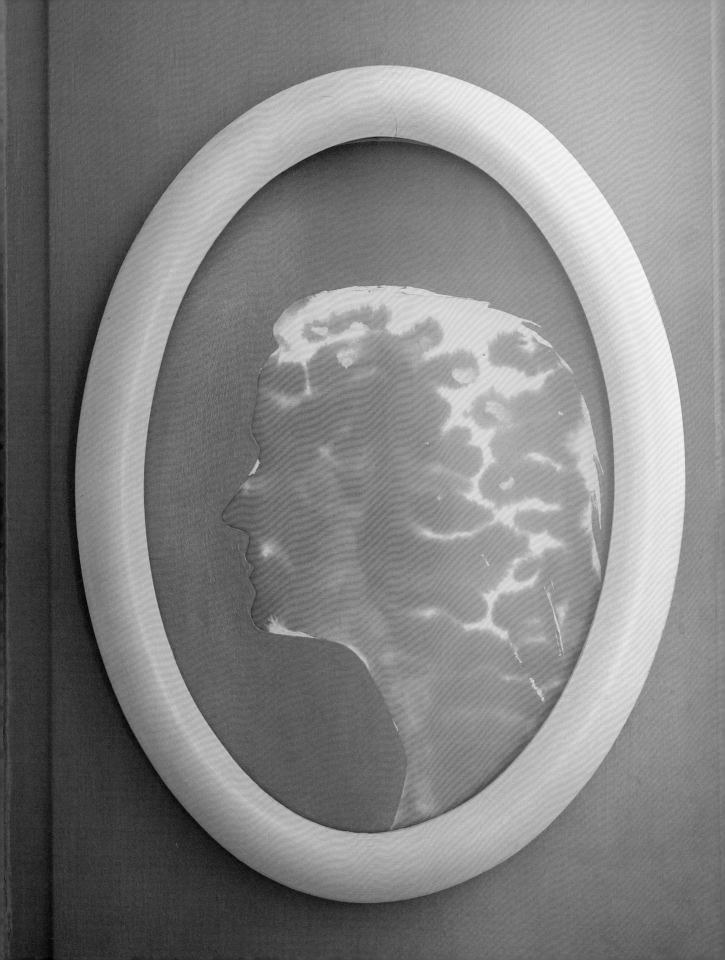

Page 13: An Icicle chandelier and table are among Antonson's first designs. The overflow of Hackett's collection of ironstone and teak bowls and trays finds a home under the chesterfield sofa.

Pages 14 and 15: Kathleen, Stephen, James, and Finn sit on the three-seater Dutch bicycle, at left, that the family uses to ferry the boys to and from school. Antonson's Shell chandelier appears to float in the living room, where his Dexter mirror and Ring lamp keep company with an extra-long armless sofa, marble-topped coffee table by Atlas Industries, and treasured found objects and flea-market finds, at right.

Pages 16 and 17: Antonson painted the silhouette of Hackett that hangs on the back of their front door, at left. Hands are a repeated theme in the couple's

life, as they are drawn to all things made with them. They found the vintage abstract painting at right in a Vermont antiques shop.

Pages 18 and 19: Plaster presides over the dining room in an Antoinette mirror, an Angele chandelier, and Volute candlesticks, all made by Antonson. The original parlor floor was covered in laminate flooring when the couple moved in; to their delight, they discovered the original pine underneath, which they stripped and coated in a light gray wash.

Pages 20 and 21: Photographs, paintings, and drawings line the wall running along the stairway to the parlor floor. The portrait of Thelonious Monk, at left, was painted by Hudson, New York, artist Earl Swanigan. A robot-painted portrait of Andrew Carnegie by artist and engineer Ken Goldberg and a flea-market oil hang on a headboard fashioned from bifold doors covered in reinforced Kraft paper and shot through with thumbtacks in a design inspired by Jean-Michel Frank.

Opposite: Antonson painted the top of the ping-pong table as if the sun is eternally shining through the trees.

Calm, Cool, and Collected

Quy Nguyen, Fort Greene

Quy Nguyen lives on the third floor of a brownstone built in 1901, which suits him to a tee, given that he is enamored of all things aged, storied, and special. "I chase the old because there's a past to unravel, a fascinating conversation to have. When you buy new things, there's not much of that," says Nguyen. A creative consultant for some of the world's top lifestyle brands, Nguyen spends his days developing and directing photo shoots of furnishings and accessories, which inevitably informs how he lives at home. "So much passes through my hands at work that I am constantly refining what I want to live with," he says. He considers himself a minimalist hoarder, rotating out pieces when he finds a better version. "I always look for the highest execution of the simplest piece. I much prefer things that have been made with the fewest possible resources. They're more interesting and to me, more beautiful."

So how does someone who describes himself as aesthetically wide open remain rigorous when it comes to living with things he loves? "I see myself as a custodian rather than a collector," says Nguyen. "It's a bit like running a museum. I put things in my home to start a dialogue." And the conversation is constantly evolving, except in the otherwise prosaic kitchen, where gleaming pots and pans are artfully arranged on the stove. The cookware tells the most personal and unchanging story; Nguyen's mother, who ran a restaurant in Saigon before it fell, refused to cook in anything but copper. "I inherited her love of cooking and her taste for beauty and quality."

Page 25: A Shaker peg rack Nguyen found at the triannual Brimfield Antique Show in Massachusetts appealed for its simple, sculptural design.

Pages 26–27: An early twentieth-century American vitrine, at left, holds stones carved to mimic constellations by the Taino people. A print by Félix González-Torres hangs over the bed, right.

This page and opposite: Nguyen cut a pair of eyes out of a book about one of his favorite artists and "wore" it as a Halloween costume. The built-in shelves in the living room, at right, hold an expertly edited selection of Nguyen's collections. "Grouping pieces by color gives clarity," he says.

28

Pages 30 and 31: Nguyen didn't want "a logical still life" on the living room mantel, left. If you remove the apple, the whole installation collapses. A pair of duckbill Windsor chairs tidily sum up Nguyen's aesthetic, at right. "They are ambiguous in terms of the period they were designed," he says.

Bohemian Rhapsody

Juliana Merz & Harry Cushing, Dumbo

"There is no plan. A plan is too static," says Juliana Merz of the primary interior design principle she shares with her partner, Harry Cushing. A quick scan of their loft, one of eighty spaces in a former munitions factory, makes it clear that the two artists practice what they preach. Who else could pull off a drippy Italian blown-glass chandelier suspended over a contemporary dining table in a room fitted out with drapes made from drop cloths? "I always envision our place as being inhabited by a decadent old lady," laughs Merz. That is, one who doesn't mind banging pipes and a little water. "We live with leaks galore—the buckets are always out—but it's worth it," says Cushing. The pair, who are as enamored of decay as they are of indulgence, say their approach boils down to just three simple tenets: scale (sometimes slightly wrong is best), contrast (put something precious next to something beautiful but worthless), and tension (pair attractive with unattractive pieces). "My best paintings are the ones that I have to make with the awful browns that are left when I run out of my favorite colors," says Merz.

Limitations fuel their creativity as much as their imaginations. "Sometimes we come up with the weirdest color scheme we can think of and try to make it work," says Cushing. "The space reminds us of a Sicilian palazzo." And they would know: Cushing was born in Rome, and Merz lived in Florence for fifteen years. These days, they decamp to Lucca each summer to escape the Brooklyn heat. "Miuccia Prada is a huge inspiration to us. She's into the whole decadent haggy look," says Merz. German director Rainer Werner Fassbinder is another influence. "Our place looks like the hotel in his film *Beware of a Holy Whore*," says Cushing. "It's a little bit ugly."

Page 33: Cushing and Merz on the roof of their Dumbo building. Of Cushing's personal style, Merz says, "He was once a bit conservative before he moved here, but all of a sudden he went wild with the glasses, sneakers, and hats. We approach dressing in the same way we do design."

Pages 34–35: "Aesthetics determine our approach to art," say the couple, who live and work among their creations. Cushing often uses text to represent forms and ideas, whereas Merz is interested in the juxtaposition of color and the movement of brushstrokes.

Pages 36 and 37: The pair, who are also interior designers, value aesthetics over trend, provenance, or price. The spare lines of a midcentury-modern chair are softened by a Swedish sheepskin rug, at left. An outsize globe of paper plates by designer Christopher Trujillo hangs over the kitchen worktable, right.

Opposite: Precious meets prosaic in the dining room, where a blown-glass chandelier that once hung in a Lucca, Italy, movie theater now alights over a B&B Italia dining room table surrounded by garden chairs. "The chandelier arrived broken, and it took us a full year to replace the pieces," says Merz.

Pages 40 and 41: A George Smith sofa sits well with a Donald Judd–inspired coffee table in the raw space, left. "We like decay, and we don't mind that the ceiling is falling down!" says Cushing. "It's so much better than a Sheetrock box." A vintage shoe rack holds art and design books, right.

Into the Woods

Evan & Oliver Haslegrave, Greenpoint

One brother is rugged, gregarious, and charming. The other is refined, reserved, and pensive. Together, Evan and Oliver Haslegrave embody the ethos of hOmE, the design firm they built from scratch in the early 2000s. Hailed as the borough's answer to restaurateurs Keith and Brian McNally, who have been credited with reinventing Manhattan's downtown, the brothers have reclaimed, reused, and recycled their way into the heart of Brooklyn's restaurant scene. With more than twenty bars, bistros, businesses, and private homes to their design credit, including Sisters, Cherry Izakaya, and Alameda, the duo is often cited as the originators of Brooklyn's DIY culture. Indeed, there was a fair amount of blood and sweat in the early years. "In the beginning, we were like sharks," says Evan. "We were so busy that if we stopped moving, we'd pass out." The home and office they shared until both recently married was merely four walls and a few columns until the pair got their hands on it. A tableau vivant of their design principles, the loft space in a gritty paper factory is as prepossessing as the brothers themselves.

Page 43: The Haslegrave brothers, Oliver (left) and Evan (right), work side by side in front of a trio of old-school doors; they map out their design concepts the old-fashioned way—on paper. "The CAD drawings come at the end, when we have to submit work to clients," says Oliver.

Pages 44–45: A pair of silk velvet–upholstered chairs bring refinement to the rough-hewn living room, where a trio of boards pulled from a Bushwick warehouse has shown up as a table or wall art in the brothers' three previous apartments. The coffee table is a transformed architect's desk.

Opposite: Materials for future projects (the mirror eventually landed at Sisters, a restaurant in Clinton Hill) are artfully stored in an alcove off the living room.

Pages 48 and 49: The original factory door that leads to the brothers' loft, left, gets a frequent makeover by neighborhood graffiti artists. A skylight floods the open kitchen the brothers built out using several of their signature "insane-scoting" cladding made from picture molding, right. They found the vintage sign at BIG Reuse in Gowanus.

Eat Play Love

Paola & Chicco Citterio, Bedford-Stuyvesant

Art, food, and family. It's the holy trinity for Paola and Chicco Citterio—or at least the secret to their ever-colorful life as artists, restaurateurs, and parents. The pair moved to New York from their native Italy for love; he for Paola's best friend twenty years ago, and Paola for Chicco, five years later. "I sold everything in my apartment in Milan to get to New York City," says Paola, who left her job as a production designer to collaborate on Manhattan's Piadina, the first of several restaurants she and Chicco would run together, most recently Lella Alimentari in Williamsburg.

Eight years ago, the couple moved to Bedford-Stuyvesant after a few years in Williamsburg, their first Brooklyn stop right after daughter Amelia was born. Her brother, Ercole, arrived four years later. "After I moved from Italy, I decided it was time to build a family, and that's where all of my inspiration comes from now," says Paola, who once punked Art Basel Miami Beach by hanging one of her hand-knotted canvases in the Pulse Gallery bathroom, then posting a citywide notice that it was missing.

Such insouciance pervades the Citterios' three-story brownstone, where an entry wall is covered in portraits the children have made of Chicco in his beloved red knit cap. "We're a very happy family because we like to play—with color, objects, and light," says Paola. She claims to be more disciplined than her husband. "Sometimes I dream about a minimal house with just a single cabinet in it, but I think it is impossible," she says. Neither has a taste for anything expensive—or serious. "You must love a mess," says Paola of her decorating approach. It's a soulful one that involves the whole family. "The kids are very much in evidence in our home. They have their own personalities that must show through. It's the combination of all of our aesthetics that makes it work."

Page 51: Art and music fill the Citterio home: *Colori Caldi*, an oil painting on felt and one of Paola's first purchases after her move from Italy, hangs between soaring parlor floor windows.

Pages 52 and 53: The Citterios favor spontaneity over formality in every part of their lives; picking up a book—or a tuba, bass, or guitar—is made equally easy from a niche in the living room, at left. After selling one of their restaurants, the couple kept the colorful Dansk enamelware, right, for their home kitchen. "We have one hundred more pieces in the basement," says Paola.

Opposite: The artist works in all versions of wool—felt, fiber, and yarn. The dining room table serves as Paola's work space. She hooked the rug inside the industrial fan cover on the wall and found the box spring into which she hooked a flower on a curb in upstate New York. "I call it *13,862 Knots and an Eviction*, because I finished it just as we had to leave our Williamsburg apartment," she says.

Pages 56 and 57: The children's homage to Chicco has become an installation on the entry wall, right. In two words, Amelia's sweatshirt, left, says it all.

Pages 58 and 59: The couple favor white walls throughout the house, introducing strong doses of color with objects and textiles instead, right. The pool green walls in the bathroom, left, are the exception.

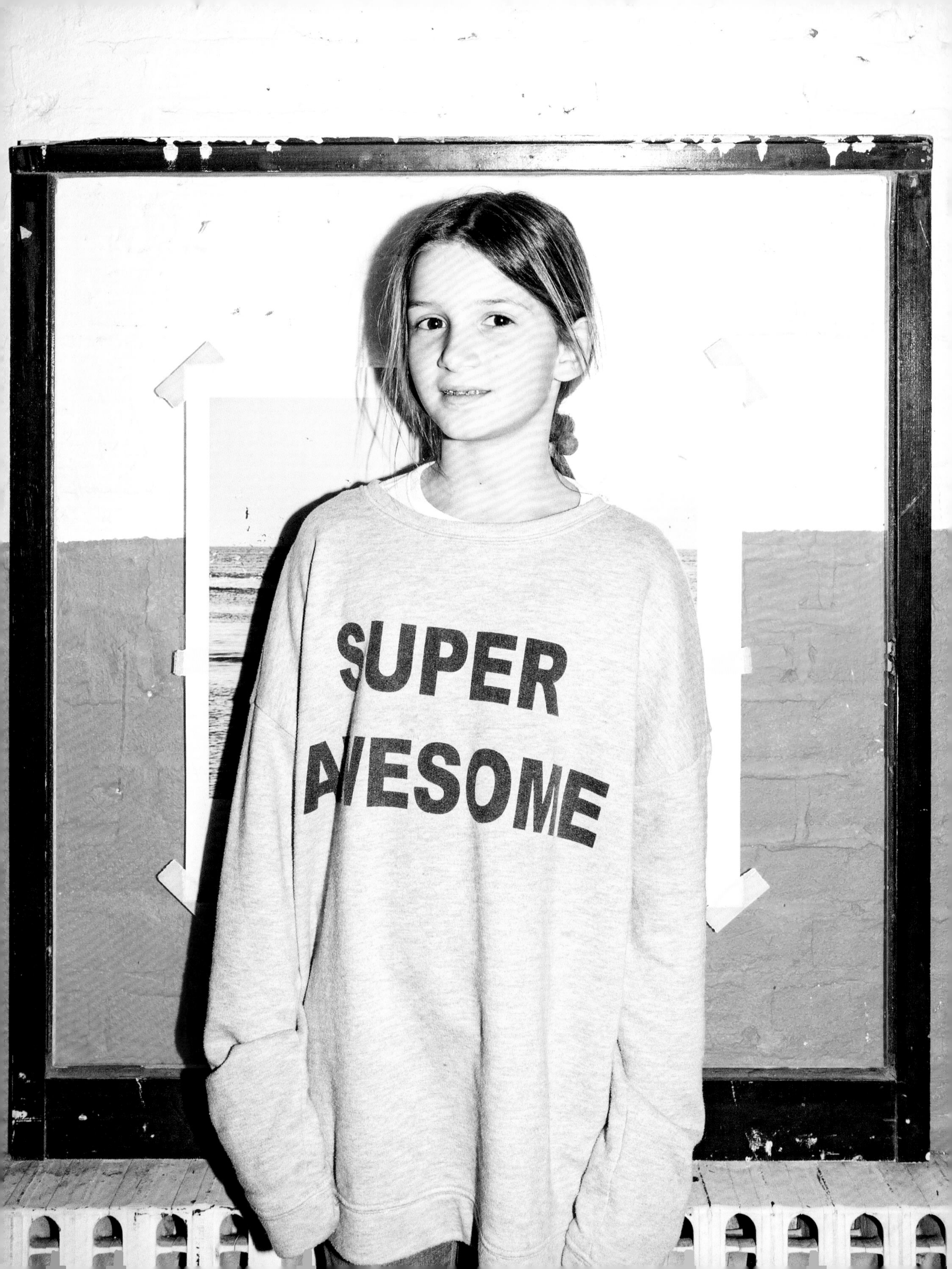
SUPER
AWESOME

Wear and Tear

Ali, Crown Heights

Multi-hyphenates are not uncommon among Brooklyn's creative types, but there is perhaps no one with more dashes in his title than mononymous fine artist–stylist–creative director–interior designer–photographer–visual merchandiser Ali. He's dropped the role that brought him to New York from Los Angeles almost two decades ago, indie record production, but the Florida-born polymath's talent for creating seems to have only intensified.

To step into Ali's loft, a live/work space in which his predilections are on full view, is to sneak a peek inside his mind. At first glance, it is expansive, serene, and considered. Spend a little more time poking around, and it's clear that this is a guy whose visual tuner is set permanently to high. And he's been that way since the tender age of eight, when a Ralph Lauren boutique opened in Ali's hometown of Tampa. "I loved to go there and just look around," he says. "All that brass, wood, and leather, and the props—they told a story." He's been creating visual narratives—in every corner of his life—ever since. Among the richest is one of his closets, a "room" in which a rack of impeccably ragged denim and workwear items—some dating back to the 1900s—serve as a wall. Put your hand on any piece, and Ali can give you the history—stitch by stitch, patch by patch, rivet by rivet. Surprisingly, his dream is to live in a furnished Frank Lloyd Wright–designed house. "You'd just have to move in with your clothes!" he says, as if he owned just a single suitcase full.

These days, when he is not working with clients of his one-man marketing concepts studio, anoblesavage.com, Ali is making paintings. "I've always had an interest in paint as a material. Its transformative properties are so powerful. And playing with pigmentation is so satisfying. Heavy, light, happy, sad—it's another medium for me to tell a story," he says.

Page 61: Full-size photocopies of vintage jeans cover one wall of Ali's studio, the beginnings of an installation he eventually exhibited. The artist sits in front of a current work, clad in his favorite Gucci loafers and a lovingly frayed boatneck wool sweater made in the 1930s.

Pages 62 and 63: Leather, feathers, and bone—a composition of unrelated objects in Ali's collection comes together in a still life on a worktable that once resided in a typewriter factory in the Brooklyn Navy Yard, right. He intentionally left the loft raw to take full advantage of its textures and patina.

Pages 64 and 65: "I've been obsessed with bags ever since I can remember," says Ali. Canvas totes, utilitarian army

bags, leather bags, backpacks, and old bank bags are all here, left. As Ali puts it, a baby grand piano case "still works—as a sculpture" in the hallway, right. The neon light fixture is by friend and artist Gandalf Gavin.

Opposite: Ali describes the shelves on one side of his closet as the collegiate collection. Vintage jerseys, rugby shirts, and sweaters bear the names and symbols of iconic American universities and clubs.

Pages 68 and 69: Ali enjoys at least two things most New Yorkers dream about: space and light, left. Architectural salvage from a turn-of-the-century brownstone becomes a backdrop for a still life in the living room, at right. It's an impromptu installation Ali created from flowers, left to dry by his friend, the artist Cara Piazza, who works with them to make natural dyes.

A Taste of India

Alayne Patrick, Carroll Gardens

Alayne Patrick swears she hasn't changed the interior of her home in the almost twenty years that she has lived there. Which is hard to believe since the native Californian has spent her entire adult life in the business of creating fashion and interior still lifes. But as a globe-trotting photo stylist in her early career, Patrick lived a nomadic life. Today, she has distilled her vision not only in her one-bedroom garden apartment, but also into Layla, a magical shop off of bustling Atlantic Avenue in Boerum Hill, a bike ride away from her home. The vest-pocket boutique is filled with antique textiles, bedding, jewelry, and printed textiles of Patrick's design cut into clothing inspired by her ongoing love affair with India.

Though neither shop nor home are much more than 700 square feet, Patrick describes her space limitations as a gift. "It's the same feeling I have about the way I dress. I have a uniform. It makes life easy," she says. And colorful. When it comes to choosing a palette, Patrick takes a page from the bazaars and markets of her adopted country. "The more colors you use, the better they work together," she says. In fact, it's the only part of her life that she doesn't keep contained. "I don't go anywhere anymore. I'm a local gal. I rarely ever leave Brooklyn," she says.

Page 71: There is nothing like a coat of red paint to revive a lackluster cabinet. Patrick used Benjamin Moore's Red.

Pages 72 and 73: Silk satin poufs, at left, from the Parisian shop Liwan are scattered around the living room. Patrick painted the whole apartment white, the ideal backdrop for dark woods and lots of bright hues, right. "It means I can bring in any color at any time," says Patrick.

This spread: A deep pink painting by Brooklyn-based artist Elliott Puckette leans on the bedside table. Patrick's collection of paintings includes examples by Riyaz Uddin, Alexander Gorlizki, and Karin Schaefer as well as a few vintage pieces.

Pages 76 and 77: Patrick pads around the apartment in Adidas gymnastic shoes, bought years ago in London. On the bench in the kitchen, at right, which Patrick traded for a little sofa she no longer wanted, she manages to make clutter stylish. The cushion is covered in an antique silk textile.

First-Person Singular

Mona Kowalska, Clinton Hill

Proper Brooklyn brownstones are coveted for many things—their finite number, spacious backyards, marble fireplaces, original floors, ornate plaster moldings, and, not least, a soaring parlor floor. Typically, this is the space into which sofas, side chairs, coffee and side tables, decorative rugs, dining room tables, and perhaps a large piece of art or two go. But Mona Kowalska has never been one to follow the herd. There's nothing but celestial blue paint on her front parlor walls. And she positioned an extra-long high bench down the middle of the room and piled it high with art books and novels. A daybed, arranged just off center along one wall, is the only seating.

It's not surprising that the fashion designer—whose cult clothing line, A Détacher, says it all—saw things differently when she moved across the East River with her daughter, Claire, five years ago. Rejecting convention comes naturally to the Polish-born Kowalska, who has staved off repeated bids to grow her company larger than the three employees she keeps. Maintaining a connection to her customers is what makes her tick.

Appliance snobbery and showpiece kitchens, however, don't. She floated an island in the middle of her kitchen and skipped wall cabinets to emphasize the striking volume of the space. In fact, Kowalska seems to be drawn to the center, a theme that runs throughout the Italianate brownstone, which she bought because it hadn't suffered any bad renovations. A worktable stretches the width of Claire's light-filled third-floor bedroom. In the master bedroom, a single stack of pillows teeters at the head of the bed.

It's all so "anonymously elegant," a phrase Kowalska uses to describe Lisbon, the only city she can imagine trading for Brooklyn. But it's just as apt a portrayal of Kowalska's singular style, not to mention the woman herself.

Page 79: Kowalska and daughter, Claire, in the front parlor of their Clinton Hill home.

Pages 80 and 81: Original pocket doors separate the front and back parlors. Not one to adhere to period details, Kowalska hung a 1970s brass light fixture, at left, from the ornate ceiling medallion. A print by Félix González-Torres hangs upside down over the fireplace. "The framer put the hook in the wrong place, and I just left it there," says Kowalska. She designed the twenty-five-pound felt tuffet, which requires shaping and adjusting to maintain its shape.

Opposite: Claire's bedroom, which serves as her studio when she's not away at art school, spans the front of the house. "I'm very fortunate to have so much light and space," she says.

Pages 84–85: The assemblage on the chest of drawers in Kowalska's bedroom perfectly captures the designer's originality. The leather choker was part of her 2011 collection inspired by neuroses. She found the oil painting on eBay and the decorative boxes in Chinatown, where they are used to package ceramics. A bunch of glass grapes holds photographs, "usually of Claire."

Pages 86 and 87: At left, in her kitchen, Kowalska emphasized the volume of the space—and chose "regular" appliances. Kowalska made the red checked pillow and bolster, at right, from a tablecloth brought back from India. She had the ikat throw made by a women's cooperative in Cajamarca, Peru. "It's the only place I have seen that knotted fringe—a perfect union of Spanish and Japanese aesthetics," she says.

82

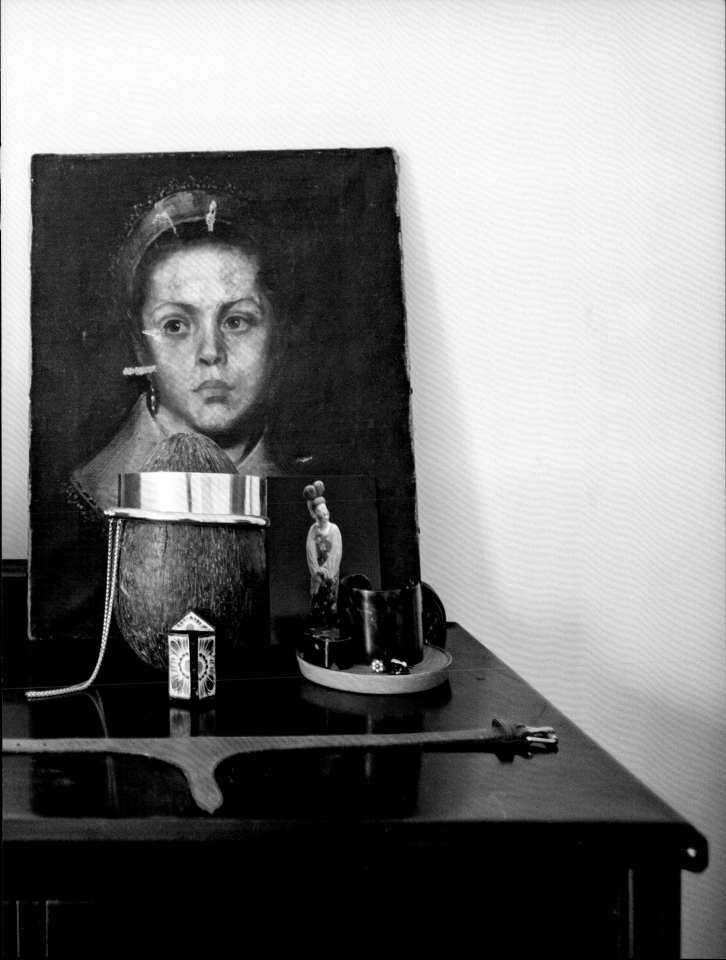

The Drama King

Carl Hancock Rux, Fort Greene

When Carl Hancock Rux's favorite salvage dealer closed up shop, he was so bereft that he showed up on the store's final day with a lit candle. "I almost shed a few tears," he says. An admitted interiors junkie, the Obie Award–winning playwright, novelist, poet, essayist, musician, actor, and radio host has a soft spot for "old things." "Pieces with history offer insight as to how people lived in a way that a book can't," he says. It's doubtful that Peggy Guggenheim ever stood at her slop sink, but Rux loves that it is now in his kitchen. Jacqueline Kennedy once worked at his dining room table, albeit when it was ensconced in New York's Society for Ethical Culture.

Rux's theatrical gifts are on full display in the Italianate brownstone he shares with his partner, Patrick Synmoie, a lawyer and gifted gardener and floral stylist. He describes his aesthetic as Gertrude Stein with an obsession with African art. "I imagine Picasso stopping by to check out a new piece Stein has bought," he says. He jokes, but Rux is constantly setting a scene. His guilty pleasure in the neighborhood is a drink at the dive bar Alibi, where there was once a player piano. "When I think about it, the bar would have been a watering hole where Henry Miller, John Steinbeck, Gertrude Stein, and Marianne Moore would meet. That place is loaded with history," he says.

Page 89: Rux is a regular at neighborhood coffee shop Smooch, where he gets the usual, a cappuccino and yogurt with granola.

Opposite: A standout on the block for the voluptuous ivy carpeting the façade, the house invites passersby to stop and stare.

This page: A nineteenth-century French mailbox serves as a wall cabinet in the kitchen, at right. An avid cook, Rux is fond of firing up his vintage turn-of-the-century enamel stove.

This spread: Rux never buys anything new; every object and piece of furniture in the living room has a story. The metal horse, stripped of its paint, once rode on a European carousel.

Pages 94 and 95: Smitten with the fresco walls he'd seen in French and Italian apartments and hotels, Rux tried his own hand at it in his bedroom, left, where a self-portrait is all that hangs on the wall. Rux purchased the eight-hundred-pound vintage tub, at right, from Olde Good Things in Scranton, Pennsylvania. "It had to be hoisted to the bathroom window by crane," he says. "The whole neighborhood came out to watch." He found the French market scale at Paris's Saint-Ouen flea market.

The Visionaries

Mats & Lorri Hakansson, Crown Heights

When Mats and Lorri Hakansson first saw the garage that they now call home, it was teeming with factory workers making antennae for cars. For less visual creatures, this might have been a problem. But a fashion stylist (her) and a creative director (him) together only intensify the desire that every visual person is familiar with; they saw what they wanted to see. "Not only were we smitten with the space, but the neighborhood was also loaded with character," says Lorri of the streets of former stables, carriage houses, and single two-story garages.

That was back in 2004, when their East Village neighborhood in Manhattan began to feel like an extension of the New York University campus. Though it's where they first met—in a bar—years earlier, the city that never sleeps had lost its allure. What was attractive was the prospect of cleaning up the garage and turning it into home.

"We saved as much as we could of the original space," says Mats of the two-story two-bedroom, two-bathroom they now share with son, Bengt, a grade-schooler, and Agi, a handsome Vischlau. They refrained from moving any walls—all the better to fit a bouncy castle into the living room—and instead enclosed the garage and mounted shelves on its back wall to create an office space. On the ground floor, poured-concrete floors waxed to a perfect sheen reflect the light that floods in from the skylight thirteen feet above. Upstairs, a central room serves as the family room, with the bedrooms and a bathroom radiating from it. When it came to furnishings, the couple agreed to keep the space spare and clean. "That was one of our rules," says Lorri. But Bengt, who has the run of the ground floor with his scooter, remembers the rule making differently. "The rule has always been that you make the rules," he says.

98

Page 97: Anchoring the living room are a pair of teal modernist chairs, which were passed down to Lorri by her grandfather. The couple renovated the skylight, which had been painted over when they moved in.

Pages 98 and 99: The pair erected just one wall in the spacious ground-floor space, turning it into an office on the inside and a garage on the backside. Bengt enjoys ample room for swinging his lightsaber without knocking over any objects (or Lorri, Mats, or Agi).

Opposite: The kitchen is tucked into an alcove just big enough to accommodate the necessities, including a generous vintage sink.

Pages 102 and 103: Waxed concrete floors run throughout the ground floor, right. Just six pieces of furniture are arranged in the living room, keeping the space open and serene. Grays abound on the second floor, at left; in the master bedroom, the richly hued walls shift colors as the day progresses.

Pages 104–105: Textures and layers—and a pair of flea market paintings—bring life to the simply furnished master bedroom.

Pages 106 and 107: The couple deployed thirteen different shades of gray upstairs, opting for the palest in the bathroom, at left, where a Murano glass chandelier and a hammered silver soap dish shine. The family room, right, features a Balinese day bed and stool along with a pair of safari chairs.

Artist's Statement

Merele Williams, Clinton Hill

"I never wanted to live in a house that was done, decorated, in a month or two," says vivacious real estate broker Merele Williams. To look around the brownstone she shares with son, Titus, and daughter, Turiya, her children with the conceptual artist and sculptor Terry Adkins, who passed away unexpectedly in 2014, one might challenge such an assertion. With its pristine white trim and walls, impeccable furniture arrangement, spot-on mix of texture, shape, and color, and utter lack of clutter, it's hard to picture this very together woman living in anything partially complete.

But Williams is no diva. When she and Adkins bought the imposing house, it was a single-room-occupancy building, with six dilapidated kitchens and holes in every ceiling. "It needed a gut renovation," she says. "And I was the general contractor." The overhaul took a full year, during which the family slept on air mattresses on various floors, depending on where work was being done.

Peeling a house back to the studs is not for the insecure; facing a shell can be daunting. But not for this couple, who knew exactly what they wanted in life and in love. "I always expected to marry an artist, so I went to an opening in a sexy red dress and met Terry, and it was love at first sight," says Williams. Adkins had long been a collector of midcentury furniture and African art, instruments, and textiles, all of which show up throughout the four-story house.

Reminders of Adkins's prodigious talents are everywhere you look. On this wall, a group of gouache botanicals in Yves Klein blue, there a thumb piano propped on the mantel. Step into the living room and you are meant to kick the pile of sleigh bells sitting next to the sofa, to fill the room with a delightful jingle. "When Terry was alive, the house was filled with music," says Williams. "I have to remember to listen to more music."

Page 108: Williams and
her daughter, Turiya, sit in
front of a group of paintings
by Lorna Simpson.

Pages 110 and 111: Adkins
poured hot glass onto a found
form, then let pieces fall off to
make the sculpture that hangs
over the mantel in the living
room, at left. Soaring between
the parlor windows, right, is a
caution-yellow staff with a
microphone attached that the
artist created for a performance
piece on the abolitionist
and shepherd John Brown.

Opposite: A photograph by
Jacolby Satterwhite looks out
onto Titus's bedroom, where
the accomplished track and
field star's medals are part of
the décor.

Pages 114 and 115: Williams is
especially fond of Adkins's series
of botanicals in Yves Klein
blue gouache; they hang over a
midcentury console in the
living room, left. A framed
Masonic mask, used in a
performance Adkins did in the
1990s, takes pride of place in
the shallow kitchen alcove, right.

Pages 116–117: In the master
bedroom, a print by Adkins is
mounted above the certificate he
received as a resident artist at
the American Academy in Rome.

THE ANTIQUE BLACKS

Sixties Radical

Joe Merz, Brooklyn Heights

Brooklyn native Joe Merz met his wife, Mary, in 1947 when both were students at the Pratt Institute in Fort Greene. Mary had spent her first two undergraduate years in Illinois, where she designed and made modular furniture for her dorm room. Encouraged by an art teacher to move to New York City, she became one of just two women in the Pratt program. "I used to kid her that I married her for her furniture," says Merz. But it was a shared love of architecture and design that initially drew the two to each other. He fondly recalls discovering that as teenagers, both had sketched and framed the same pencil drawing from a textbook by an artist who, it later turned out, would be their professor at Pratt. Theirs was a match made from graphite and paper.

Mary Merz passed away several years ago, but her legacy lives on in the home she and her husband designed in 1965 for themselves and their four children (see daughter Juliana's loft on page 32). One of three unmistakable Merz collaborations on a street lined with brownstones and brick townhouses, the concrete-block structure recalls the work of Louis Kahn, one of Joe's strongest influences. "Back then, the neighbors were very mixed about what we were doing because the houses were so radically different," he says. But context is everything, and the couple was lauded by the American Institute of Architects for their sensitivity to the scale of their surroundings. Inside, the ghost of Frank Lloyd Wright—and a love of nature—pervades the rooms. "Mary was deeply inspired by Wright, but she was equally passionate about the outdoors," says Merz.

Page 119: The painting hanging over a Joe Merz–designed dining table is a board game painted by his daughter, artist Katie Merz.

Pages 120–121: The architects designed niches in the kitchen wall in order to provide storage and an appealing view from the living room.

This page and opposite: After their four children were grown, the Merzes converted the third and fourth floors into an apartment furnished with midcentury-modern pieces, left. Merz, standing in the garden, at right, designed the windows in the back of the house to mimic those in the front.

The Perfect Canvas

Karin Schaefer & Diane Crespo, Brooklyn Heights

Tucked away in the master bedroom of a classic six, city real estate parlance for a prewar apartment of as many rooms, Karin Schaefer sits in front of an easel making the paintings that have earned her multiple residencies at the Josef and Anni Albers Foundation. Her pieces, made with minuscule paint strokes, are reflective of the rest of the space she shares with filmmaker Diane Crespo and their son, Kaya. Atmospheric, serene, and meticulous, the couple's home, like Schaefer's art, is a series of color fields floating on a neutral canvas.

"Karin is the neatnik," says Crespo. Not that Schaefer lacks a playful side. In fact, she and Crespo lead decidedly lighthearted double lives. As the founders of Acorn, a toy store so entrancing it soothes even the most frazzled city nerves, the pair have created a retail space that looks like what Schaefer might have designed for her six-year-old self. "I grew up in England, Holland, and Germany, where wooden and felted toys were common," says Schaefer, a former Waldorf teacher. Nature, too, was a heavy influence. Schaefer tries to bring as much of it into the apartment as possible, in a way that Crespo gleefully describes as obsessive. "At the beginning of each summer, she announces that we are only collecting a certain color rock. Last year, it was brown," Crespo laughs.

Page 125: Schaefer describes Brooklyn as if it were turn-of-the-century New York. "It's the kind of place people imagine classic New York to be."

Pages 126–127: The long view from the dining room through to the living room gives Schaefer a change in perspective after sitting at the easel in her bedroom studio.

Opposite: Schaefer completed *Trouble the Water*, an oil on panel, in early 2015. Nature plays a pivotal role in Schaefer's design aesthetic.

Pages 130 and 131: Old-school is cool in the galley kitchen, at left, where a pegboard reminiscent of Julia Child's organizing system puts the cook's tools at her fingertips. On one of several salon walls, right, this one over Schaefer's desk, is a collection of black-and-white works, including Inuit wood-block prints, a Tomoko Daido photograph, and drawings by Stephen Johnson and Schaefer.

Scenes from a Marriage

Becca Abrams & Nathan Benn, Brooklyn Heights

"I'm going to marry you" were among the first words Nathan Benn uttered to Becca Abrams. That was twenty-five years ago, when Benn, a photographer for *National Geographic*, met Abrams on a photo shoot for the magazine. They've been together ever since. Finding love—and keeping it—is a challenge for most mortals, but when passion is mixed with colliding aesthetic obsessions (early American furniture for him; contemporary photography for her), what are the chances?

In their apartment overlooking Brooklyn Bridge Park, Benn and Abrams, along with their son, Tobias, and smooth fox terrier, Webster, live among brave, if unlikely, unions. Works by Sally Mann, Katy Grannan, and William Wegman are set against traditional patterned wallpaper by such venerable houses as Brunschwig & Fils and Colefax and Fowler in rooms filled with important eighteenth- and nineteenth-century furnishings. But Benn and Abrams seem to relish audacious moves. After almost fifteen years on Manhattan's Upper East Side, they sought open sky and a view of the water. Leaving a classic prewar apartment for a white box didn't faze the couple one bit; they tapped the Ralph Harvard design firm to give the space gravitas, then called on interior designer Richard McGeehan to make it feel like home. "There's no best way to live, but Brooklyn comes pretty close," says Abrams.

Page 133: A photograph by Katy Grannan hangs on a wall papered in Kanchou in Verdigris by Colefax and Fowler. The sofa, upholstered in a silk velvet, is by George Smith.

Pages 134 and 135: Just months after arriving in Brooklyn, Abrams marveled that she was invited to join a stitching group of members "at least a decade older" than her. Her pillow, at left, is among a collection on the living room sofa. Benn's passions are captured in the entrance to the living room: a coveted Boston slipper chair sits adjacent to his own photograph, at right, of Jamaican sugarcane workers each wearing several hats.

Opposite: Webster's favorite spot is atop a nineteenth-century quilt on an early nineteenth-century Federal-style reeded four-poster bed. Sally Mann's *The Wet Bed* and a photograph by Benn hang over it.

Pages 138–139: Benn, left, and Abrams wearing masks by master mask maker Ida Bagus Anom purchased on their honeymoon in Bali, Indonesia. The moldings and details in the living room were very closely modeled on Colonial rooms at Winterthur, where Abrams says Benn would choose to have his ashes spread.

Page 141: The Zuber wallpaper in the powder room was created in the 1920s for traditional tastes but departed in scale from the typical allover designs of the period. The couple presciently had it mounted on canvas in their previous apartment so they could take it with them should they move.

*fire on the head,
fire in the bed...*

Smoke and Mirrors

Stephen Drucker, Park Slope

As a teenager, native New Yorker Stephen Drucker spent every weekend apartment hunting with his parents. "There were no open houses with panicked mobs in those days. Everybody was moving to the suburbs," says Drucker. "Instead, there were lots of empty glamorous new apartment buildings with desperate landlords." He considers the endless home search during those impressionable years as the central drama in his life. Indeed, while building a journalism career in Manhattan that would take him to the top of some of the best-selling lifestyle and interior design magazines in the country, Drucker moved nineteen times.

At twenty, the hunt just may be over. "My first comment when I saw the Brooklyn apartment was, 'Ah, the Grand Concourse,'" says interior designer Tom Scheerer, referring to the similarly fancy Bronx boulevard where Drucker grew up. "He was coming home, in a sense," says the designer. Scheerer managed to respect the space's old New York vibe, if not its nostalgic pull on his client, while creating the contemplative space Drucker wanted. "Never once did he mention the words *fabulous* or *glamorous*," says Scheerer. Rather, the classic one-bedroom is an ascetic lair with a bit of film noir running through it—the Remington has been replaced by a laptop, which can be tucked away. Drucker, who holds a degree in historic preservation, has been pulling it out daily, however, to work on a book about his adopted borough.

Page 143: Drucker achieved his vision of a place of retreat and contemplation from the minute he walks into the foyer, where a Saarinen table is the only piece of furniture.

Opposite: A pair of nineteenth-century English taborets sits beneath *Smoke Rings*, a six-foot-square photograph by Donald Sultan from the Mark Humphrey Gallery in Southampton, New York.

Pages 146–147 and 149, top: No teetering stacks on this coffee table. A pair of nineteenth-century French urns keep company with essential reading. Instead of curtains, Scheerer had screens papered over with a Fornasetti wallcovering.

Pages 148 and 149, bottom: Drucker found the oak kitchen cabinet, at left, at one of his favorite haunts, Ruby Beets, in Sag Harbor, New York. It holds part of his collection of Wedgwood drabware and basalt. The 1920s wooden clock, right, he found at Heal's in London. "It ticks loudly, and the kitchen just doesn't feel right unless it's ticking," he says.

A Great Catch

Maura McEvoy, Dumbo

One of Maura McEvoy's lasting teenage memories is of blowing her first pay-check from waitressing at an antiques store. On scrutinizing her take, her beloved grandfather said only, "A fool and his money are soon parted." But McEvoy, a professional photographer and former photo stylist, has always gone with her gut—not least of all in real estate—and it has rarely defied her.

Over the past decade, the enviable view from the loft she shares with her daughter, Oona, has changed dramatically. "There was nothing here but deserted warehouses. It was incredibly isolated, as if time had forgotten it," she says of Dumbo. Her neighbors in the former toilet-seat factory have resided there for forty years. Today, the sprawling park out front teems with bicyclists, brides, flaneurs, young families, hipsters, and everyone in between.

Despite the neighborhood's remarkable resuscitation, strolling around isn't as alluring to McEvoy as nesting is when she's home; the demand for her talents takes her away for weeks—sometimes months—at a time. Not that she's a shut-in. Roaming around her loft offers up the best kind of armchair travel. "Everything in this apartment fell off a prop truck or came from a flea market," she laughs. Filled with furnishings, objets, and curiosities discovered on or inherited from far-flung assignments—as well as found closer to home at the Brooklyn Flea—the loft tells the story of McEvoy's globe-trotting life, one chair, scroll, shell, throw, vase, stone, and postcard at a time. "The spontaneous finds are always the best. And who cares if they're the real thing?" she says.

Page 151: Oona taped the spoon to the wall after her mother asked her not to put this particular piece of flatware in the dishwasher. "She called it her 'art,'" says McEvoy.

Pages 152–153: A surfboard that has been in the McEvoy family for decades anchors a corner of the living room. Mementos from near and far sit on a sideboard there. McEvoy brought the Chinese scroll back from her first travel assignment, during which she photographed ten different cities around the world in a single month.

Opposite: McEvoy and Oona at home on a lazy Sunday.

Pages 156–157: McEvoy peeled back all evidence of the former bachelor pad—complete with sunken living room with a dais running around its rim and curvaceous walls—to expose the bones of the loft.

KGR.
ENGLAND

Hzm.
Lothringen

Hzm. Fran

KGR.
FRANKREICH

Hzm.
Schwab

KGR.

BURGUND

Korsika

L'evenement
BANAL
Une Aventure
RACONTER

Whiteout

Hans Gissinger & Jenni Li, Cobble Hill

Walls may talk, but it's a white floor that tells the true story of how a family lives. In the home of Hans Gissinger and Jenni Li, the worn, painted pine boards in the kitchen say it all. This is a couple who cooks for family and friends as often as possible, flawless floors be damned. When Li, a Peruvian-born fashion stylist, and Swiss photographer Gissinger moved into their brick row house in 2013, they painted it top to bottom in Benjamin Moore's Super White. It was a bold choice, given the couple's two boys, Harmony and Son, were crayon-wielding toddlers at the time. "A coat of bright paint was the easiest way to 'renovate' the space," says Li. It also made for a seamless transition of their furniture, which has stood the test of seven moves since the couple met. "I just change its purpose to suit the space," says Li.

There was a time, however, when Li's line of thinking was at odds with her lifestyle. When she lived in Manhattan, she would walk past the Antony Todd store every day on her way to work. "I so desperately wanted to make my space look as effortlessly elegant as he made his," she says. In the end, she couldn't bring herself to live in a place that looked good but was impractical for the way she lived. "A great interior makes you feel good in it. I needed a 'Come in and kick your shoes off' kind of home," she says.

Keeping a simple, minimal interior is Li's idea of eliminating stress and chaos in her family's life. Not that color hasn't crept into every corner of the house. Bright feather mobiles made by Li's teenage daughter, Taylor, hang from the ceiling; fluorescent tape holds up the children's artwork; Peruvian pom-poms hang from doorknobs; painted Indonesian cabinets show up here and there; and the bold stripes of a Hudson Bay blanket invade the all-white piano room. "Somewhere in my aesthetic, there's a longing for color," says Li.

Page 159: Gissinger's photograph of an exploding cake, part of a series, hangs in the entryway. Neutrals inspired by nature—shells, stones, bones—make up the predominant palette throughout the house.

Pages 160 and 161: Mr. and Mrs. Feathers, left. The kitchen island, at right, was a dinner table in a previous apartment; Li added casters and a marble top to better suit the open space.

Opposite: Gissinger and Li, seated to his left, love a crowded dinner table, including the family parakeets and Noah, their maltipoo. Li designed the chandelier, a steel rim lined with self-adhesive LEDs, and had it fabricated locally.

Pages 164–165: Gissinger shot the black-and-white sky as well as the unframed photograph of Li and her daughter that leans atop the piano, a Craigslist find.

Pages 166 and 167: Apart from a coat of Benjamin Moore's Super White and a few towel hooks, Li left the bathroom walls bare; the vintage cast-iron tub came with the house. A stump hauled back from a weekend in upstate New York serves as Son's bedside table. Gissinger fashioned the reading light from a stick and a clamp fixture.

Pages 168 and 169: Pom-pom garlands from Li's native Peru inject a jolt of color in the master bedroom, left. Along one kitchen wall, storage and laundry seamlessly blend to create a backdrop for the boys' artwork, right.

Old Soul

Anne O'Zavelo, South Park Slope

The only reason Anne O'Zavelo returns to her native Ireland is to visit her mother. "I moved to New York City specifically because it is an antidote to my homeland's melancholy," she says. The lawyer, novelist, interior designer, and café owner has lived stateside for more than twenty-five years, with all but two of them in Park Slope. "I don't like preciousness," she says. "I'm a little bit masculine in my approach because I'm rugged. That's why Brooklyn is a perfect place for me." Indeed, the borough has O'Zavelo to thank for its pair of quintessentially European cafés, Café Regular and Café Regular du Nord, both in Park Slope. She's also the design force behind the beloved coffee shop Little Zelda and the bar Two Saints in Crown Heights.

In the "poor man's version of a brownstone" that she shares with her husband, lawyer Don Zavelo (her maiden name is O'Connell, from which she borrowed the *O'* in her name), her two sons, Oliver and Myles, and Lola, a standard poodle, O'Zavelo has created the kind of home she'd longed for throughout her childhood, which was largely spent at boarding schools. "I always coveted other peoples' homes," she says. "I was always taking notes." Her observations—a fireplace is essential, proportion is key, and editing is a must—sit well with middle-schooler Myles. He's so happy in his house that it's hard to coax him out the door each morning. "Why would I ever leave?" he says. "It's so great here."

Page 171: O'Zavelo stenciled *OLmy Social Club* on her front door, the first two letters of her sons' names and a joke at her own expense. When her boys were in elementary school, snagging playdates became nearly impossible once it got out that O'Zavelo and her husband practiced laissez-faire parenting. She kept the phone numbers of the precious few in a folder titled the same on her computer.

Pages 172–173: To achieve the putty walls in Myles's bedroom, O'Zavelo had it painted several times. "The first few tries were way too red, so we kept toning it down," she says. The linen duvet cover is from The Red Threads in Manhattan. She had the dry cleaner down the street stitch the headboard cover.

Pages 174 and 175: "Dressing up is inseparable from design," says O'Zavelo, who has a penchant for couture and designer heels. She opened her first coffee shop, Café Regular, at right, just a few steps from her house because she wanted a wonderful place to sit. "It's a third place," she says.

Opposite: A graphic painting by friend and artist Bill Tresch hangs on the stairway landing wall, which is painted in Benjamin Moore's Witching Hour. O'Zavelo chose a palette that works with the imperfections of the house. "Everything is old and cracked and probably wasn't the best quality when it was built," she says. "I also went for color that minimizes the dingy factor and works well with dust, movement, and light."

Double Vision

Robert Highsmith & Stefanie Brechbuehler, Cobble Hill

Two light-filled rooms sandwich a third in Stefanie Brechbuehler and Robert Highsmith's parlor-floor apartment. It's a common arrangement as brownstone rentals go, but it presents a design dilemma nevertheless. "Each room here has, at one time or another, been a dining room, living room, or bedroom," says Highsmith. Most mortals would move the sofa, dinner table, and bed in and call it home. But when design and architecture course through the veins of both husband and wife, playing musical rooms is a form of relaxation.

In 700 square feet, the couple has managed to create a home that embodies the ethos of Workstead, the firm they cofounded upon moving to Brooklyn from Manhattan in 2009. "We are fascinated with materials that have older associations but are used in a more inventive way," says Brechbuehler, who is also a jewelry designer. That is certainly the case with the Wythe Hotel in Williamsburg and the Arcade Bakery in Manhattan, as well as their many residential projects.

Their home is ostensibly spacious, spare, and warm, an aesthetic combination that can elude the less disciplined among us, but these two have genetics on their side. Highsmith hails from three generations of architects, while Brechbuehler's Swedish lineage includes stonemasons and craftsmen. Despite the calm, the pair does feel the need to flee to their upstate farmhouse on the weekends. It's just 950 square feet, but that's intentional. "Our plan is to live a big life on a small scale," says Highsmith.

Page 179: A Potence lamp by Jean Prouvé hangs in the living room, where the furnishings hail from family (Eames chair), the street (sewing table chopped down to a coffee table), and Ikea (sofa, on which the couple replaced the legs.

Pages 180–181: Brechbuehler and Highsmith installed the shelving and designed the chandelier in the dining room. The shelf lights are vintage factory lamps by Dazor.

This page and opposite: The couple intentionally keep the bedroom spare, as it is in the middle of the floor-through layout, where it is quiet and dark. Ivy frames the view from the dining room out to the backyard, at right.

182

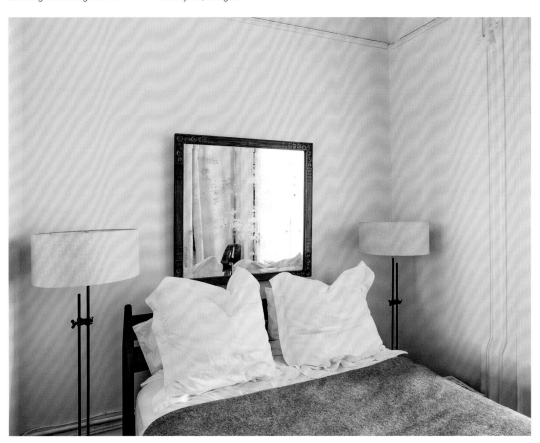

Pages 184–185: A neutral palette, natural materials, and disciplined design choices highlight the flow of air and light in the 700-square-foot space.

Finders Keepers

Victoria & Nick Sullivan, Boerum Hill

Interior designer Victoria Sullivan pedals around the neighborhood on her Dutch bicycle clad in shoes better suited for the runway. Fashionable, yes, but fearless is more accurate. Six years ago, Sullivan moved with her husband, Nick, the fashion director at *Esquire* magazine, their then three-and-a-half–year-old daughter, Florence, and eight-week-old son, Charlie, from a London townhouse to first a duplex rental and finally to the brick row house that is now home. "The shipping container arrived when I was out of the house, and by the time I came back, Nick had arranged all of our things," she says. It was no small feat, given the pair's enviable magpie spirit.

The Sullivans tore the building back to the studs and rebuilt it (Victoria served as general contractor) before they got to the fun part. Behind every piece of furniture, lamp, painting, and pillow in the brick row house, there's a tale of rescue, reinvention, or good old-fashioned romance. This is a pair with the pluck to place on the mantel a painted bust of Joseph Stalin—who's smoking a cigarette dispensed from the tail of a plastic elephant (which was won in a game of bingo). The children dragged home the living room table—a curbside find—in a Radio Flyer. The bullhorn in the foyer came from a nearby shop specializing in tattoos, piercings, and curiosities. A Murano glass vase recalls a memorable day at London's Portobello Road.

The Sullivans feel right at home in their neighborhood, where on any given Saturday, they ply the stoop sales, in which residents sell off the contents of their closets and basements on the front steps. "I am out there patrolling the streets, looking for the chalk signs on the sidewalks," says Victoria. The thrill of the hunt never wanes. "Sometimes we think about decluttering, putting it all in a box," she says. "But every single piece has a story."

Page 187: Nick, Victoria, Charlie, and Florence Sullivan in front of their restored row house.

Pages 188–189: Benjamin Moore's Quiet Moments covers the walls in the front parlor, where Sullivan paired a Queen Anne writing desk she inherited from her father with a ghost chair. She found the egg chair at a stoop sale.

Pages 190 and 191: Why not tuck a photograph of Twiggy and a souvenir fan, left, into the edges of a gilded frame? The study, at right, just beyond the front parlor, is saturated in a Ralph Lauren nautical blue.

Pages 192 and 193: Victoria aged a new Union Jack by staining it with tea, then dragging it through a mixture of mud and gray paint, right. A smoking Joseph Stalin presides on the mantel in the study, left.

Opposite: A collection of prints, photographs, and paintings along with a framed skeleton mask from a Halloween party line the foyer wall.

Pages 196 and 197: All that remains from the original house is the clawfoot tub. The shutters are a street find that Sullivan spray-painted white. "They actually fit!" she says. The Queen's Guard lines the shelves in Charlie's bedroom, left.

Mayflower Mad

Matt Austin, Bushwick

Matt Austin grew up in a home that has been in his family for more than two hundred years. Patina, earned or created, makes him tick. As a teenager, he made replicas of early American candle boxes and passed them off to the local antiques dealer as heirlooms from his grandmother's attic. "If he offered to buy them, I knew I had succeeded, which is all I wanted to do. I never sold them, of course," says the artist and designer, who is trained in seventeenth-, eighteenth-, and nineteenth-century French and American lighting. Youth was not wasted on the adolescent Austin, however. He managed to parlay his predilection for playing tricks on the eye into a thriving career. He once painted all the walls in a Marc Jacobs boutique to look like plywood in just three days.

Austin's railroad apartment is equal parts homage to his heritage, New England thrift, alchemy, and Mr. Magorium's Wonder Emporium. Here, there's a gilded elephant on wheels with magnetic wings. There, an old pipe box holds sketchbooks. The slate backsplash in the kitchen is made from discarded chalkboards that hail from Yale University, where Austin once worked. The streets of Brooklyn are also a design resource. "I get a lot of parking tickets, so I steal stuff like police barricades from the city in the deepest parts of Brooklyn and turn it into construction material for my apartment." He even manages to make his beloved racing bike—Austin is an internationally ranked cyclist—look like sculpture. But perhaps his most cunning design move lies underfoot. Eight hours before his fortieth birthday party, Austin realized he needed a special dance floor, so he painted one in a favorite pattern seen in various squares in Lisbon. He invited guests to what he affectionately calls his "penthouse walk-up" to christen the new floor. "Their shoes scuffed it up in the most perfect way," he says. "They didn't realize they were working for me."

Page 199: Austin carved the serpentine studies and hand-mixed the ocher and French gray paint for the walls in his bedroom.

Pages 200–201: A winged articulated pendant light, one of Austin's most popular designs, hangs over an antique blanket chest. He carved the cod presiding over the cannonball bed, a family heirloom.

Pages 202–203: Austin adopted the local footwear when he was making art in northern Holland several years ago. On returning to New York City, Austin painted spats on them. "When I moved in, the kitchen was abhorrent," says Austin, who used plywood and slate to transform it, along with a collection of nineteenth-century push-up brass candlesticks, right.

This page and opposite: The patterned floor, left, recalls the black basalt–and–white limestone mosaic pavements in some European cities. A collection of pieces by the ceramist Eric Bonnin and a lobster claw, a gift from Austin's father as a reminder of their lobstering outings on Long Island Sound, are on display in the kitchen, right.

Pages 206–207: The artist was abroad on an art fellowship on September 11, 2001. He made the painting *King Kong Was Wrong* in the twenty-four hours that followed, left. A collection of carved-wood hat molds, inspired by nineteenth-century French papier-mâché, watch over the kitchen table, right.

Next Wave

Victoria & Richard Emprise, Red Hook

When the eponymous furniture and accessories company founded by Victoria and Richard MacKenzie-Childs was surreptitiously sold out from under them, the couple lost everything (they have since changed their last name). They found themselves living in a tiny one-room apartment in a former hotel on Manhattan's Upper West Side with their beloved wirehaired dachshunds, Mr. Brown and Pinkie. "We used to joke that we could open the refrigerator door with our toes and have breakfast in bed," says Victoria. Such humor, along with the pair's artistic temperaments, was key to finding their eventual home aboard the century-old *Yankee*, the last remaining ferryboat to shuttle immigrants from Ellis Island to the mainland as well as the only one to have fought in both World Wars. "Whenever we are given a challenge, we never look at it as a heavy burden. We think of it as an opportunity, as having infinite possibility."

The couple survived two moves with the *Yankee*—from her original home in lower Manhattan and a stint on the Hoboken, New Jersey, waterfront to docking for good in Red Hook. "Living on a boat is like an eternal camping trip: exhilarating but hard, hard work," says Victoria. Naturally inclined to create environments around them, the artist couple never once considered going the nautical route with the *Yankee*. "You step onto her, and you go someplace in your heart," says Victoria. Indeed, to cross the gangplank is to go down the rabbit hole. "We once thought of the *Yankee* as our home, studio, and place of refuge, but we realize now she doesn't belong to us. We're just her stewards for now," says Victoria.

Page 209: Rescued from a marine salvage yard in Providence, Rhode Island, in 1990, the *Yankee* was restored by her previous owner and subsequently placed on the National Register of Historic Places. The duo has created the Yankee Ferry Foundation, through which they invite companies to hold off-site meetings or retreats aboard.

Opposite: Victoria and Richard in the "living room."

Pages 212–213: "Richard and I have a folk talent, a natural inclination to create environments," says Victoria. In the living room, they've combined bold striped, checkerboard, and floral patterns reminiscent of their former company's aesthetic.

Pages 214 and 215: Vintage lanterns light the dining room in the cabin, left. No basic bunks on this ship; a cabin for young overnighters, at right, is fitted out with a theatrical touch.

Arts and Letters

Tim Hunt & Tama Janowitz, Prospect Heights

It is fitting that novelist and short-story writer Tama Janowitz and her art-dealer and collector husband Tim Hunt elected to live in one of Brooklyn's grandest buildings, an Art Deco gem with a beautifully restored lobby. The author of *Slaves of New York*, the pop lit phenom that defined downtown Manhattan's art milieu in the 1980s, and her British husband, a longtime curator of Andy Warhol's estate, together make a head-turning pair. She with the pile of wild hair, flame-red lipstick, and colorful couture and he, a dapper devotee of bespoke clothing, can hardly avoid making a grand entrance.

For almost twenty years, Janowitz and Hunt have resided in a penthouse apartment with enviable 270-degree views from a wraparound terrace. It's about as far from trendy Manhattan, not to mention hipster Brooklyn, as it gets. Sixteen floors up, the couple has filled the classic prewar three-bedroom with an idiosyncratic mix of art, textiles, and books collected over decades. Janowitz, who decamps upstate with daughter, Willow, for extended periods of time to care for her ailing mother, was never tempted to live in a Brooklyn brownstone—too dark. Instead, she and her family live in light-filled rooms that deliver on the promise the listing for the place made all those years ago, one that the denizens of *Slaves* could never have imagined. They have their castle in the sky.

Page 217: In the living room, a sculpture by Tom Bell looms large over an unorthodox selection of seating and a Jeff Koons' ceramic vase.

Pages 218 and 219: A series of self-portraits by John Waters hang above Hunt's Heywood Wakefield desk and 1960s Italian chair, left. The trio of iron objets trouvés are part of a larger collection. Sofas draped with Brazilian textiles, at right, keep company with works by Francesco Clemente, Larry Rivers, Dumitru Gorzo, and Picasso.

This spread: Color, shape, and form come together on a Heywood Wakefield sideboard in the dining room: a handle for a rice-harvesting knife from Myanmar, a meteorite fragment, and a piece of ancient Chinese jade sit below works by sculptor Sidney Geist and Russian artist Alyona Kirstova.

True Colors

Agnethe Glatved & Matthew Septimus, Ditmas Park

Preservationists have their place, but it isn't in the home of Agnethe Glatved and Matthew Septimus. Having lived in a house full of dark wood floors and moldings prior to moving into their current five-bedroom Colonial Revival, the couple bathed every room in a blizzard of white. Such light-seeking makes sense; she's Norwegian and he is a photographer. "I love looking at the bright winter light in the living room. It reminds me of home," says Glatved, who came to New York to study at the Parsons School of Design, where she met her husband.

When the couple purchased the house, in a neighborhood of freestanding homes built after the railroad to Coney Island was completed in 1885, it hadn't been updated in half a century. But the creative director in Glatved saw what others couldn't: its good bones and generous windows were obscured by layers of curtains and sickly paint colors. The pair replastered all of the walls and fixed all of the floors. "I don't think we would have dared embark on such a big project had we not been familiar with these houses," says Septimus. The results are as colorful as the family of four themselves. Most of the action takes place in the kitchen, where daughter Nora and son Ezra do their homework while Glatved and Septimus, an accomplished cook and pizzaiolo, prepare dinner. But there's a spirited feeling in every room, where all that white is suffused by a playful use of color. "Matthew and I traveled to India many years ago, and it completely changed the way we look at color," says Glatved. Though her Scandinavian sensibility prevails, she insists her husband has equal say. "But we're both pretty stubborn," she laughs.

Page 223: *Some Acts of Everyday Life*, a multi-panel painting by the artist Jill Vasileff, spans a wall in the living room.

Pages 224–225: All of the artwork in the house is by close friends or Septimus, who shot the two photographs on the bookcase in India. A pair of red chairs gifted to the couple sit among those designed by Hans Wegner.

Opposite: Color invades a corner of the living room, where a pair of sculptural vintage folding chairs keep company with Jill Vasileff's *Pink Hum* and a Danish felt ball rug by Hay. The collage in the alcove is by Erica Harris.

Pages 228–229: The home's original coffered ceilings were covered up when the couple first moved in. "We wanted a kitchen that both was modern and showed off the architecture," says Glatved. The collection of ceramic tableware is primarily by Gleena.

Pages 230 and 231: Left, Ezra, Agnethe, Matthew, and Nora gather in the keyhole alcove in the master bedroom. In one corner, painted sawhorses from IKEA and a piece of plywood make a simple desk, right.

Pages 232–233: The couple never intended to leave the walls in their top-floor bedroom empty, but waking up to the light and bare surfaces won out. The landscape paintings are by John Dubrow.

Page 10, clockwise from top left: Paola and Chicco Citterio (page 50) serving up dinner to friends at Celestina. In Stefanie Brechbuehler and Robert Highsmith's (page 178) kitchen. The Haslegrave brothers' (page 42) loft. Mona Kowalska's (page 78) daughter, Clare. The live/work studio of Harry Cushing (page 32). A street find in Victoria and Nick Sullivan's row house (page 186). Jenni Li and Hans Gissinger's (page 158) son Harmony made the multicolored skull.

Page 11, clockwise from top left: Maura McEvoy shares her Dumbo loft (page 150) with her daughter, Oona, whose bedroom reflects her inherited aesthetic. Mats and Lorri Hakansson (page 96) did up their son Bengt's bedroom in a strong, vibrant palette. Maura McEvoy (page 150) created a wall collage of museum postcards in a corner of the kitchen. The Haslegrave brothers (page 42) outside their Greenpoint loft. CD storage in Juliana Merz and Harry Cushing's Dumbo loft (page 32). The view from Stephen Drucker's Park Slope apartment (page 142).

What We Love

In my early years as an interior design writer, I spent far too much time focusing on pillow shapes, sofa styles, and wall covering choice—and precious little on the homeowners who live with them. Funny, as I am and always have been infinitely more interested in the people who inhabit these interiors, in the ineffable connection they have to their surroundings, and what aesthetic choices they make beyond their living rooms. As the years passed, I began to use the subject of interior design as an entree to the richer stories in people's lives—or at least as access to a great cache of sources and resources to add to my own little black book. I love knowing what makes people tick, what brings them joy, where their passions lie. I thought you might, too.

Stephen Antonson and Kathleen Hackett
Boerum Hill (page 12) FUEL: Blue Bottle in Boerum Hill for the cold-brew New Orleans coffee and the Americano. Little Zelda in Crown Heights when we are in the neighborhood. FOOD: Black Mountain Wine House in Carroll Gardens or Vinegar Hill House in Vinegar Hill in the winter. Steamed clams at the Fish House and maple walnut ice cream from the Novelty on Monhegan Island, Maine, in the summer. A picnic in the Place des Vosges in Paris anytime. LARDER: We are never without Greek olives, tzatziki, and fresh cashews and almonds from Sahadi's in Cobble Hill. Bien Cuit in Boerum Hill bakes bread and pastries to perfection. SHOP: The Marston House and Trifles in Wiscasset, Maine, and Pierre Passebon's Galerie du Passage and Marché aux Puces de la Porte de Vanves in Paris. BHV, the Parisian hardware store. P.S. Bookshop in Dumbo for excellent used art and design books. VISIT: The Clyfford Still Museum in Denver, Colorado. Single-artist museums allow you to go deep—you get to see the evolution of his wonderful paintings. The fabulous plaster pieces in the Egyptian galleries at the Brooklyn Museum. TRAVEL: Anywhere that requires a ferry to reach it. IF NOT BROOKLYN: Bonnieux in the south of France.

Quy Nguyen
Fort Greene (page 24)
SHOP: It's nice to walk up and down Atlantic Avenue. I like Holler & Squall a lot because the people who run it are lovely. FUEL: The Annex Coffee Shop. They make a delicious pastry with sausage and goat cheese and flawless scones and muffins. BROWSE: The books are beautifully presented at Greenlight Bookstore. And you can sit and read for five hours and nobody minds. EAT: Battersby is perfect: the scale, the lighting, the food, the service. Hibino is my favorite place for Japanese food. They make the most beautiful soy pudding. LARDER: I go to Provisions. Is that bad to say? It's so expensive.

Juliana Merz and Harry Cushing
Dumbo (page 32)
FUEL: Double espressos at Brooklyn Coffee Roasters or the same at AP Café in Bushwick. FOOD: King Noodle in Bushwick for everything vegan. The music is too loud for us old folk, but the food is worth it. Whole Foods in Gowanus has changed our lives. We've sold out. VISIT: The Palais de Tokyo in Paris, not only for the exciting and refreshingly non-trendy work, but also for the spectacular deconstructed interiors. Life on Mars gallery, in Bushwick, because of their dedication to the community. Gagosian Gallery in Manhattan. SHOP: Any thrift store. In Williamsburg, Pilgrim because it's a surf shop. Permanent Records and Earwax Records for vinyl and Cosmo for junktiques. Vintage shopping at the mercatini dell'antiquariato in Italy's Renaissance towns for great rugs, lighting, jewelry, and vintage sunglasses. And eBay, because purchasing used things alleviates the guilt. WATCH: Rainer Werner Fassbinder's *The Marriage of Maria Braun* and *The Bitter Tears of Petra Von Kant*. "Marriage changed my perspective on art and what it could be," says Cushing. Of Tears, Merz says, "He presents the garish as beautiful. It's a low-budget masterpiece."

TRAVEL: India, for its physical, philosophical, and mystical beauty—and we're hooked on Iyengar yoga. IF NOT BROOKLYN: Paris in the winter, Italy in the summer.

Evan and Oliver Haslegrave
Greenpoint (page 42)
FUEL: An Americano from Homecoming (Evan) and an espresso from Cookie Road (Oliver), both in Greenpoint. LIVE MUSIC: Sisters (Oliver) in Clinton Hill. QUIET: WNYC Transmitter Park at the end of Greenpoint Avenue (Evan and Oliver). SALVAGE: Any thirty-yard dumpster (Evan); the sidewalk (Oliver). EMBARRASSING BUT TRUE: I like Starbucks (Evan); I love the G train (Oliver). Dream Design Job: A beer bar in the Alps would be really cool. IF NOT BROOKLYN: Lots of places. Do we get a mansion? (Evan); wherever we get a mansion (Oliver).

Paola and Chicco Citterio
Bedford-Stuyvesant (page 50)
LARDER: The Red Hook Fairway. I get emotional when I park my car in their lot. I love the color of the water and the smell of the air. Of course, I love the warehouses because there's a lot of rusty iron stuff around. EAT: Marlow & Sons in Williamsburg. We have been going there for coffee every morning for the last ten years. They leave the exact same amount of room for milk in the cup every time. We're angry now, though, because a couple recently stole our corner table. IF NOT BROOKLYN: There is no magic place. Everywhere! My dream is to travel and never stay in one place too long. One day,

we might buy an Airstream and drive wherever we want to go.

Ali
Crown Heights (page 60)
BRUNCH: Sun in Bloom in Park Slope. It's a gluten-free, vegan, and raw restaurant. Get the biscuit with gravy and shiitake bacon. And the orange and ginger juice. DINNER: The Pickle Shack in Gowanus has the best barbecue pulled oyster mushroom sandwich. BOOKS: The Strand in Manhattan has always been a favorite. ART: The Larco Museum in Lima, Peru. The courtyard is amazing. The art at the Barnes Foundation in Philadelphia is beautifully put together. The textures, colors, and moods are wonderful. MUSIC: House of Blues and jazz at the World Stage, both in Los Angeles. Summer concerts in Central Park are also pretty great. IF NOT BROOKLYN: Definitely a city that I don't have to drive in. London interests me. So does Lima. Maybe Tokyo? Brazil?

Alayne Patrick
Carroll Gardens (page 70)
FOOD: Yemen Café for the salads, baba ghanoush, and ful medames. Vinny's for chicken soup. SHOP: Erie Basin in Red Hook for the best antique and vintage jewelry. FILM: Cobble Hill Cinemas for its size and location. GUILTY PLEASURE: A Pink Poodle at Brooklyn Farmacy & Soda Fountain. It's hibiscus soda with vanilla ice cream and seltzer. Or a big bowl of hot chocolate with whipped cream at home, in bed, on a cold night.

Mona Kowalska
Clinton Hill (page 78)
FUEL: I order Leftist Espresso

Blend from gimmecoffee.com and make it at home. FOOD: Locanda Vini & Olii on Gates Avenue in Clinton Hill. It's very adult in there. I don't feel like the oldest person in the room. SHOP: The Brooklyn Flea in Fort Greene, in particular the Japanese guys who sell men's clothes. It's all-American stuff as seen through their eyes. LARDER: The greenmarket in Fort Greene Park is the perfect size and a nice long walk from my house. VISIT: Coney Island at 4 p.m. in the summertime. Or in the dead of winter, when it feels like Odessa, Ukraine. Take the train and it's as if you've really gone somewhere else. The light is so beautiful there because of the water.

Carl Hancock Rux
Fort Greene (page 88)
DREAM PERFORMANCE SPACE: I've performed pretty much all over the world, but the Paris Opera was one of my greatest highs. I'd love to be invited to the Austin City Limits Live at the Moody Theater. That would be really special. SHOP: The Chelsea Garden Center in Red Hook. They call the plants "she." The Puerta de Toledo flea market in Madrid is the best for finding vintage brass and ceramics, among other things. STROLL: Right near my neighborhood on Clinton Avenue to look at the Pratt mansions and Waverly Avenue to look at the carriage houses. GUILTY PLEASURE: A drink at Alibi. The cheesecake at Junior's. I should stay away from it. All of Dumbo. I love it, but I am embarrassed a bit by the new-money chic. IF NOT BROOKLYN: Marseille. It's the Brooklyn of France. Beauty, grit, and a multicultural crowd.

Merele Williams
Clinton Hill (page 108)
SCENT: Le Labo's Jasmin 17 in the warm months and Rose 31, also by Le Labo, in the winter. Both are simply lovely. SEE: The Tate Modern in London. I love it because the artworks are diverse. Plus, they purchased an incredible work, Muffled Drums, by my late husband. They just get it, the world, the diaspora. FUEL: I hate coffee and only drink tea. My favorite is Steven Smith Teamaker's Lord Bergamot—made at home. EAT: Roman's on DeKalb is just a few blocks from my house. Andrew, the owner, really appreciates his clientele. I love the pureed chickpeas with kale or spinach, especially the olive oil they pour on top. SHOP: The Sablon Antiques Market in Brussels! It's full of incredible antiques and objets. It's beautiful. My favorite clothing stores in the world are Zero + Maria Cornejo on Bleecker Street in Manhattan and Duro Olowu on Masons Yard in London. Both of them make my life easy and wonderful. I always look great because of them, except when I exit Tangerine Hot Power Yoga in downtown Brooklyn. Thank you, Tamara Behar! READ: Jhumpa Lahiri's *The Lowland*. Apparently she lives one neighborhood over, but I have never met her. IF NOT BROOKLYN: Rome. I lived there for a year with my family when Terry was at the American Academy, and it was the happiest year of my life.

Joe Merz
Brooklyn Heights (page 118)
STROLL: Mary and I spent a lot of time in the early years of our marriage visiting the Brooklyn Botanic Garden looking for exotic plants. We turned the top floor of the house into our own version. EAT: Rose Water Restaurant is connected with a little farm, so the food is very fine and fresh. There are no more than thirty seats; it's quiet and lovely. Also, al di la Trattoria, which takes me straight back to Italy.

Karin Schaefer and Diane Crespo
Brooklyn Heights (page 124)
STROLL: We're happy to talk about Brooklyn Bridge Park to anyone who will listen.

Hans Gissinger and Jenni Li
Cobble Hill (page 158)
SHOP: The Five and Diamond vintage clothing shop in Hudson, New York. I have a weakness for '50s dresses, most of which sit in my closet because I cling to the hope that one day my waist will shrink to the midcentury silhouette. And what's not to love about Barneys and Bergdorf—you can find everything under one roof. But I'm not afraid to say great things can happen when you mix in a piece from Zara or H&M. TRAVEL WITH KIDS: If you asked them, they would choose any holiday that involved a large hotel with a pool, breakfast buffet, room service, and TVs and telephones in the bathroom. Tumbes, on the Pacific in northern Peru, is my choice. Locally, we ride bikes along the greenway to Louis Valentino, Jr., Park and Pier in Red Hook. It never gets old. FOOD: Peruvian food is, in a word, delicious. But I have long been a fan of Alice Waters, and after following her for nearly fifteen years, I finally had the privilege of eating at Chez Panisse. There is no better food in the world.
EMBARRASSED TO ADMIT: We rarely use Prospect Park! I guess we move toward the water instead. LARDER: The Borough Hall farmer's market, Staubitz Market for meat, Fish Tales for seafood, Stinky Bklyn for cheese, Smith & Vine and the Brooklyn Wine Exchange for wine. It's all within five or six blocks. TREAT: Blue Marble for ice cream. It's as good as it gets. Café Pedlar for the pain au chocolat. One Girl Cookies is our go-to for birthday cakes, but their cookies, cupcakes, and whoopie pies are great any day. It's an ideal playdate stop. They're all in Cobble Hill.

Anne O'Zavelo
South Park Slope (page 170)
ESCAPE: A long run in Prospect Park. It reminds me why I live here. FUEL: Café Regular, I have to say. EAT: Franny's. I love the food, and there's a kind of community there. Runner & Stone and The Pines in Gowanus are great too. Il Buco on Bond Street in Manhattan (food and design like it is still 1987) and El Blok in Vieques, Puerto Rico, for food and design. SEE: I love going to the Brooklyn Academy of Music. Even if the film is not so great, being in that space elevates the experience all the way around. SHOP: I found an Eames chair and table at Time Galleries here in Park Slope for practically nothing. I happen to spend a lot of time at Rick Bettinger's Antiquities & Oddities in Kansas City. It's three blocks of disassembled buildings and all of their fixtures. INSPIRED INTERIOR: I love the Hotel @ the Lafayette

in Buffalo, New York. Strangely, given my own home, I am most drawn to the midcentury style—all the usual suspects and also the unsung ones all over the suburbs, especially in the Midwest. The Robin Walker houses in Ireland and Eileen Gray house in France are also favorites.

Robert Highsmith and Stefanie Brechbuehler
Cobble Hill (page 178)
FOOD: Lucali for pizza, any table at Vinegar Hill House and the window table at Black Mountain Wine House for dinner, and Strong Place for dollar oysters! Chez Moi is charming. Dassara makes the best ramen with a sous vide egg! Iris Café is our Thursday night haunt; we eat there before leaving town to go upstate. FUEL: The best cup of coffee is on the deck of our country house in the Hudson Valley. Can't beat it! SHOP: Tartaix, a hardware store in the Marais in Paris. For clothes, Totokaelo in Seattle is amazing, and Diane T. in Cobble Hill has a wonderfully edited selection of women's clothing. It's intimate, and the service is great. For furniture, BDDW is stunning. Oliver Gustav in Copenhagen has a gorgeous selection of unique lighting and sculptural objects. It's impossible to pick one! DREAM HOME: Villa Necchi Campiglio in Milan. Architecture: Venice. The entire city.

Victoria and Nick Sullivan
Boerum Hill (page 186)
EAT: Rucola is our favorite neighborhood place. Our Friday ritual is dinner at Frankies Sputino. Brooklyn Crab is brilliant for shrimp and margaritas. SHOP: Eva Gentry Consignment. It's reasonable, and they always have great shoes—Jimmy Choo and Giuseppe Zanotti—that are hardly worn for a great price. DRINK: The Long Island Bar is divine. Lavender Lake is full of young people and has good pub food, and we can cycle home. We generally stay in our house during the day and go out at night. IF NOT BROOKLYN: Harbour Island, in the Bahamas, without question.

Matt Austin
Bushwick (page 198)
STROLL: Green-Wood Cemetery. My parents used to take me camping in Mennonite cemeteries. FOOD: Café Ghia. The menu is always changing, and they make a great burger. FUEL: I really like my own coffee. I use Café Bustelo and an old Italian espresso maker. VISIT: The Onderdonk House. A beautiful example of eighteenth-century architecture in Ridgewood, Queens. The Metropolitan Museum of Art. It's far better than seeing a therapist. At my lowest, I always come out of there happier. Kremer Pigments in Manhattan. If you want to know how to make all-natural pigments or dyes, this is the place. IF NOT BROOKLYN: Iceland or the French Alpes-Maritimes, where the Alpe d'Huez climb is the single most difficult bicycle climb in the world. Or the Connecticut River Valley. It's so connected to the land; it's private, proper, and liberal.

Agnethe Glatved and Matthew Septimus
Ditmas Park (page 222)
FUEL: Four & Twenty Blackbirds for coffee and the most amazing pie. They sell whole pies first-come, first-serve, and they go fast. EAT: Mimi's Hummus—the shakshuka is great for brunch. We love Di Fara pizza, despite the hour wait for a $5 slice of pizza lovingly made by the 75-year-old owner. LARDER: Every weekend Matthew drives to Bensonhurst and buys ravioli at Papá Pasquale's, and cold cuts, sausage, and olive oil at Frank & Sal's. Abroad, we love the food markets of Nice, France. Everything there reminds us what food should taste like. STROLL: The Long Meadow in Prospect Park is wonderful in all seasons. We got married there! Our beloved old dog's ashes are sprinkled on a tree there, too. SPECIALTY STORE: Layla's textiles and linens are a feast for the eyes. Collyer's Mansion has wonderful home goods. The obscure independent books and magazines at the MoMA PS1 bookstore. SEE: The Polar Bear Club swim on New Year's Day at Coney Island. It's the funniest Brooklyn scene, with a crazy mix of people. PHOTO OP: People's faces on the streets of Brooklyn. There is every nationality and skin color in the world. IF NOT BROOKLYN: A modern wood cabin in Norway overlooking the sea.

ACKNOWLEDGMENTS

First and foremost to Stephen. Thank you for, well, everything.

Hilary and Agnethe, your artistic gifts go without saying. Your friendship, humor, and generosity kept me going.

Matthew, kudos for gamely taking this on—and bringing your infant daughter along on occasion. I will babysit anytime.

As agents go, Carla Glasser is among the greats—rational, wise, and funny.

As editors go, Chris Steighner is among the best kind—smart, stylish, steady, and patient.

As publishers go, Charles Miers at Rizzoli, whom we affectionately refer to as the Wizard of Oz, is among the finest.

There would be no book were it not for the people featured on these pages. I found them all the old-fashioned way—through colleagues, friends, friends of friends, and the homeowners themselves. Thank you all, for opening your doors, sometimes at the least convenient times for you, and giving us the full run of your homes.

Thank you, Mary Ann Young, for being that sister—clever, witty, gifted, and kind. You will always be my kind of interior designer.

There are dozens of friends who do not appear in this book but who contributed in intangible ways. You know who you are. Thank you.

First published in the United States of
America in 2016
by Rizzoli International Publications, Inc.
300 Park Avenue South
New York, NY 10010
www.rizzoliusa.com

© 2016 Kathleen Hackett

Photographs © 2016 Matthew Williams
Design by Agnethe Glatved and Maria Stegner

2016 2017 2018 2019 / 10 9 8 7 6 5 4 3 2 1
Distributed in the U.S. trade by Random
House, New York
Printed in China
ISBN-13: 978-0-8478-4745-7
Library of Congress Control Number:
2015953474